# Evidence Based Practice in Education.

*Teaching Strategies for the Reflective Teacher.*

*Written and Edited By Paul Stevens-Fulbrook.*

*With contributions from Oliver Caviglioli*

*Cover design by Caitlin Budgen*

# Introduction.

WIth so many learning theories and education fads popping up all the time, it's hard to know what we should and shouldn't be doing right?

Wouldn't it be better if there were strategies out there based on actual research?

At least we would know we can trust them rather than believing something that is either taught to new teachers because that's how it's always been done or following a fad because it's made an impact on social media/in the staff room/someone made it up to further their career.

Don't get me started on "learning styles"!

Luckily, there is a swathe of evidence based teaching practices that are gaining a lot of momentum.

I have written about the most relevant and useful ones on my website ([teacherofsci.com](teacherofsci.com)) and have employed many of the ideas in my classroom. The results have been frankly profound, both for me and my students.

They are not whole ethos changes, they are not, for the most part, that new and they are most definitely backed up by lots of juicy evidence.

On reading this short book, you may find yourself thinking "well, this is just common sense" or "I already do this". That's exactly what I was thinking as I was researching them.

Well, they are...and yes, you probably do do some of them. I know this because you are a great teacher. I know you are a great teacher because you are sitting wherever you are reading this, you are trying to improve your practice...that already sets you apart from those who soldier on blindly, not thinking about evolving as the classroom evolves around them.

However, if you open yourself up to these theories and start to think about how they do or do not apply to how you teach now, you'll start to see very pleasing changes (and probably a reduction in workload...jackpot!).

# Rosenshine's Principles of Instruction.

Barak Rosenshine's "*Principles of Instruction*" has been gaining a lot of attention in the UK over the last year, and rightly so. However, it doesn't seem to have made any waves anywhere else.

That's a lot of teachers missing out on what I believe is the single best piece of education theory out there!

It is easy to assimilate because it helps you streamline and organise your teaching using skills you already have.

By the end of this section, you'll be buzzing to get back into your classroom! But keep reading, there's a lot more to whet your appetite.

## Who was Barak Rosenshine?

Barak Rosenshine was born on August 13th 1930 in Chicago, Illinois.

He was a high school history teacher originally but stopped actively teaching in 1963 to gain a PhD in Education at Stanford University. After completing his PhD he taught at Temple University for 2 years before moving to the University of Illinois.

It is at the University of Illinois that he taught educational psychology and published many papers, mainly focusing on teacher performance, direct instruction and strategies based on cognitive science.

Whilst at Illinois, Rosenshine first proposed his instructional teaching functions, on which he based his later work on the principles of instruction.

## Rosenshine's Six Instructional Teaching Functions.

In 1982 and again in 1986 (with Robert Stevens), Rosenshine, laid out six "*instructional functions*".

These functions were determined from prior research of successful teacher training and student achievement programs.

Rosenshine and Stevens looked for commonality between the studies they used. They filtered all their observations down into the following six instructional functions:

1. Review, checking previous day's work (and reteaching if necessary).
2. Presenting new content/skills.
3. Initial student practice (and check-ing for understanding).
4. Feedback and correctives (and re-teaching if necessary).
5. Student independent practice.
6. Weekly and monthly reviews.

Rosenshine didn't intend this paper to be the final word on instructional functions, more as an opening gateway to further research. As Rosenshine himself said:

> "*There's no hard fast dogma here. It is quite possible to make a reasonable list of 4 or 6 or 8 functions; however, these functions are meant*
>
> *to serve as a guide for discussing the general nature of effective instruction*".
>
> Rosenshine, B. (1982) *Teaching Functions in Instructional Programmes*. National Institute of Education. Washington DC

## Roseshine's Principles of Instruction.

As a teacher myself, I recognise that a lot of the pedagogical texts that trainee teachers are presented with have either been superseded or, even worse, debunked as [educational myths](). While some offer a good basis of guidance, they can be confusing (at least I found them so when I was training).

What we should be teaching new teachers isn't only (or, even) [Vygotsky](), [Piaget]() and [Bloom](), but something that makes more sense, is more relevant and something that is based on actual research.

Where on Earth would we find such pedagogical genius?

Well, it turns out it's been here, in various forms, all along.

In my teacher training, it took me countless hours pouring over Piagetian and Vygotskian theories, trying to work out what on the hell they were talking about. Have they led me to teaching superpowers?

No.

In truth, I haven't paid them much thought in the 8 years since.

It took me 20 minutes to read Rosenshine's 2012 paper.

I gained more from that 20 minutes than the sum total of the teacher training research hours/days/millennia (it certainly felt like millennia).

**It takes Rosenshine just 9 pages to deliver the golden fleece of pedagogy.**

## So what is it all about?

The principles of instruction identified by Rosenshine are taken from three areas of research:

- **Research in cognitive science.**
- **Research on the classroom practices of master teachers.**
- **Research on cognitive support to help students learn complex tasks.**

Rosenshine found, that while several of the principles were evident in more than one of the above areas of research, none were contradicted.

Given that all three, very different areas of research supported and complimented Rosenshine's principles, we can be more inclined to accept their validity.

Like all good Science, his theory has been subject to modification as new understandings were reached.

## Rosenshine's 17 Principles of Effective Instruction.

In a paper published in 2010 by the International Academy of Education (IAE); "*Principles of Instruction*", Rosenshine expanded on his original list of 6 ideas. These 17 principles were collected from the 3 areas of research above.

1. **Begin a lesson with a short review of previous learning.**
2. **Present new material in small steps with student practice after each step.**
3. **Limit the amount of material students receive at one time.**
4. **Give clear and detailed instructions and explanations.**
5. **Ask a large number of questions and check for understanding.**
6. **Provide a high level of active practice for all students.**
7. **Guide students as they begin to practice.**
8. **Think aloud and model steps.**
9. **Provide models of worked-out problems.**
10. **Ask students to explain what they have learned.**
11. **Check the responses of all students.**
12. **Provide systematic feedback and corrections.**
13. **Use more time to provide explanations.**
14. **Provide many examples.**
15. **Reteach material when necessary.**
16. **Prepare students for independent practice.**
17. **Monitor students when they begin independent practice.**

# Rosenshine's 10 Principles of Instruction.

Two years after the IAE paper was published, Rosenshine published a further, revised edition of the paper; "*Principles of Instruction: Research-based Strategies that Teachers Should Know*".

In this paper, Rosenshine had, for the sake of clarity (I believe), simplified the list of principles, from a rather ominous 17 down to a more manageable and less intimidating 10.

1. **Begin the lesson with a review of previous learning.**
2. **Present new material in small steps.**
3. **Ask a large number of questions (and to all students).**
4. **Provide models and worked examples.**
5. **Practise using the new material.**
6. **Check for understanding frequently and correct errors.**
7. **Obtain a high success rate.**
8. **Provide scaffolds for difficult tasks.**
9. **Independent practice.**
10. **Monthly and weekly reviews.**

## 1 Begin the lesson with a review of previous learning.

Rosenshine suggests investing 5-8 minutes to review previous learning. This can be in the form of questioning techniques to check understanding and to uncover and challenge misconceptions, peer or self-marking work and correcting mistakes. This will strengthen understanding and the connections between ideas.

## 2 Present new material in small steps.

Presenting new information in small, bite-sized chunks increases the progress made by the students. Introducing too much at once will see progress rates fall as they can only process so much at one time. This reduction in cognitive load allows metacognition to take place (it allows them to think about how they are thinking about the task).

## 3 Ask a large number of questions (and to all students).

Questions are a teacher's most powerful tool, they can highlight misconceptions, keep a lesson flowing and challenge students to think deeper into a subject. The greatest value of questioning though is that they force students to practice retrieval, this strengthens and deepens memory.

## 4 Provide models and worked examples.

Delivering new information to students by linking it to something or some process they are familiar with allows students to gain an understanding quicker, it also gives them deeper retention. This is especially true of more conceptual ideas.

In Science, we may explain the flow of electrons in a circuit by using the model of the water in a "lazy river". The water being the flow of electrons, the pumps providing the voltage (power) and the people in the water providing resistance.

## 5 Practise using the new material.

Practice makes perfect right? Rosenshine postulates that this is true of physical, vocal and mental practice. He suggests that successful teachers allow more time for guidance, questioning and repetition of processes. Actually, in teaching, I prefer to use the phrase "Practice makes Progress".

## 6 Check for understanding frequently and correct errors.

Regular asking of direct questions (rather than "does anyone have any questions?") allows teachers to check a classes/student's understanding and catching misconceptions, therefore informing the teacher whether any parts of the topic need reteaching.

## 7 Obtain a high success rate.

[Teaching for mastery](#) ensures all students in a class are ready to move on to the next stage in the topic, thus preventing students from taking misunderstanding into their future learning.

From his research, Rosenshine found that a class that the optimal success rate is an 80% understanding. This shows that not only have the students learnt the material but also were challenged in doing so. Any higher and the work may not have been challenging enough and vice versa.

## 8 Provide scaffolds for difficult tasks.

When introducing a more difficult lesson, Rosenshine suggests employing [Vygotskian scaffolding](#). Providing students with a framework that more easily allows them to make progress.

The scaffolds can then be gradually removed as their competency grows. Examples of scaffolds can include; checklists, cue cards or writing frames. Teachers can also anticipate commonly made errors and build tools into the scaffold tasks that reduce the chances of students making the same mistakes.

## 9 Independent practice.

Following scaffolded tasks, students should be competent in the task and therefore can practice the task independently. This repetition of the task will promote a deeper fluency, Rosenshine called this "overlearning".

## 10 Monthly and weekly reviews.

An extension of the first principle, monthly and weekly reviews of previous learning aids recall of information and processes.

# THE PRINCIPLES OF INSTRUCTION

## TAKEN FROM THE INTERNATIONAL ACADEMY OF EDUCATION

This poster is from the work of Barak Rosenshine who based these ten principles of instruction and suggested classroom practices on:

- research on how the brain acquires and uses new information
- research on the classroom practices of those teachers whose students show the highest gains
- findings from studies that taught learning strategies to students.

### 01 DAILY REVIEW

Daily review is an important component of instruction. It helps strengthen the connections of the material learned. Automatic recall frees working memory for problem solving and creativity.

### 02 NEW MATERIAL IN SMALL STEPS

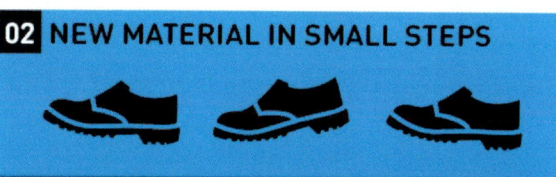

Our working memory is small, only handling a few bits of information at once. Avoid its overload — present new material in small steps and proceed only when first steps are mastered.

### 03 ASK QUESTIONS

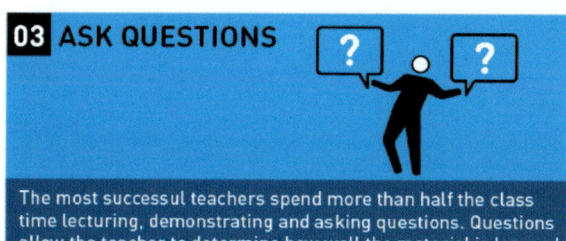

The most successul teachers spend more than half the class time lecturing, demonstrating and asking questions. Questions allow the teacher to determine how well the material is learned.

### 04 PROVIDE MODELS

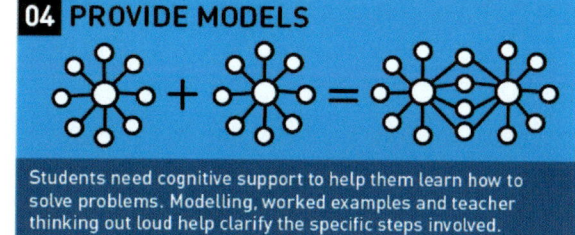

Students need cognitive support to help them learn how to solve problems. Modelling, worked examples and teacher thinking out loud help clarify the specific steps involved.

### 05 GUIDE STUDENT PRACTICE

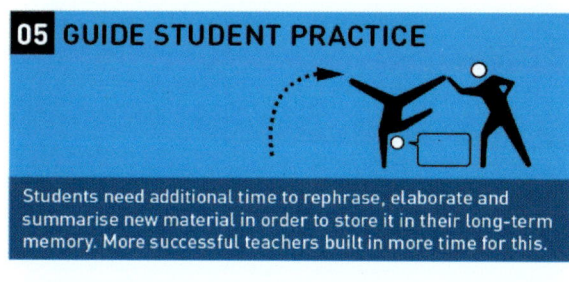

Students need additional time to rephrase, elaborate and summarise new material in order to store it in their long-term memory. More successful teachers built in more time for this.

### 06 CHECK STUDENT UNDERSTANDING

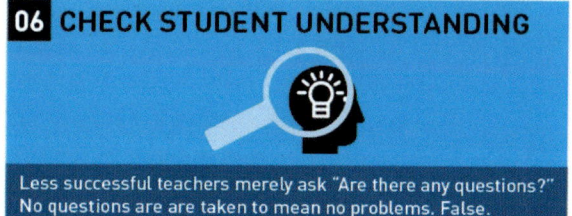

Less successful teachers merely ask "Are there any questions?" No questions are are taken to mean no problems. False. By contrast, more successful teachers check on all students.

### 07 OBTAIN HIGH SUCCESS RATE

A success rate of around 80% has been found to be optimal, showing students are learning and also being challenged. Better teachers taught in small steps followed by practice.

### 08 SCAFFOLDS FOR DIFFICULT TASKS

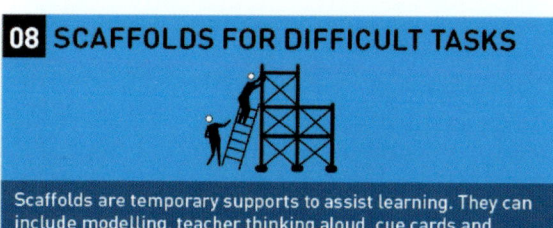

Scaffolds are temporary supports to assist learning. They can include modelling, teacher thinking aloud, cue cards and checklists. Scaffolds are part of cognitive apprenticeship.

### 09 INDEPENDENT PRACTICE

Independent practice produces 'overlearning' — a necessary process for new material to be recalled automatically. This ensures no overloading of students' working memory.

### 10 WEEKLY & MONTHLY REVIEW

The effort involved in recalling recently-learned material embeds it in long-term memory. And the more this happens, the easier it is to connect new material to such prior knowledge.

# Tom Sherrington: Rosenshine's Principles in Action.

Ex Physics teacher, author and education consultant, Tom Sherrington has become the go-to expert on Rosenshine's Principles.

He has written about it at length on his blog ([teacherhead.com](teacherhead.com)) and his recent short book; "[Rosenshine's Principles in Action](Rosenshine's Principles in Action)" takes Rosenshine's already excellent paper and makes it even more accessible for today's teachers.

> "My admiration for Rosenshine is largely informed by my experience working with teachers in various schools and colleges where I've been trying to engage people with research in order to support them to improve their practice. For me, it is the best, most clear and comprehensive guide to evidence-informed teaching there is."
>
> Tom Sherrington. teacherhead.com

## Tom Sherrington's Four Strands.

In Tom's analysis of Rosenshine's 10 Principles of instruction, he proposes grouping them into 4 strands that combine connected principles. Sherrington then orders the four strands into a workflow of a lesson.

### Strand 1: Sequencing Concepts and Modelling.

SEQUENCING CONCEPTS & MODELLING

❷ Present new material using small steps     ❽ Provide scaffolds for difficult tasks

❹ Provide models

**Strand 2: Questioning.**

⸺⸺⸺⸺⸺⸺⸺○ **QUESTIONING** ○⸺⸺⸺⸺⸺⸺⸺

❸ Ask questions    ❻ Check for student understanding

**Strand 3: Reviewing Material.**

⸺⸺⸺⸺⸺⸺⸺○ **REVIEWING MATERIAL** ○⸺⸺⸺⸺⸺⸺⸺

❶ Daily review    ❿ Weekly and monthly review

**Strand 4: Stages of Practice.**

Sherrington is quick to point out that Rosenshine's work is NOT a checklist that needs to be included in every lesson, but more as a framework that encourages teacher development.

**Barak Rosenshine's PRINCIPLES OF INSTRUCTION**

A thematic interpretation for teachers by **Tom Sherrington** @teacherhead

VISUALISED BY OLI CAV Oliver Caviglioli @olicav

## ○ REVIEWING MATERIAL ○

**❶ Daily review**   **❿ Weekly and monthly review**

Daily review is important in helping to resurface prior learning from the last lesson. Let's not be surprised that students don't immediately remember everything. They won't! It's a powerful technique for building fluency and confidence and it's especially important if we're about to introduce new learning — to activate relevant prior learning in working memory.

## ○ QUESTIONING ○

**❸ Ask questions**   **❻ Check for student understanding**

The main message I always stress is summarised in the mantra: ask more questions to more students in more depth. Rosenshine gives lots of great examples of the types of questions teachers can ask. He also reinforces the importance of process questions. We need ask how students worked things out, not just get answers. He is also really good on stressing that asking questions is about getting feedback to us as teachers about how well we've taught the material and about the need to check understanding to ensure misconceptions are flushed out and tackled.

## ○ SEQUENCING CONCEPTS & MODELLING ○

**❷ Present new material using small steps**   **❹ Provide models**   **❽ Provide scaffolds for difficult tasks**

Small steps — with practice at each stage. We need to break down our concepts and procedures (like multi-stage maths problems or writing) into small steps that each be practised.
Models — including the importance of the worked-example effect to reduce cognitive load. We need to give many worked examples; too often teacher give too few.

Scaffolding is needed to develop expertise — a form of mastery coaching, where cognitive supports are given — such as how to structure extended writing — but they are gradually withdrawn. The sequencing is key. Stabilisers on a bike are really powerful aids to the learning and confidence building — but eventually they need to come off.

## ○ STAGES OF PRACTICE ○

**❺ Guide student practice**   **❼ Obtain a high success rate**   **❾ Independent practice**

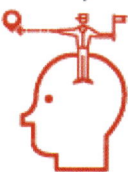      

Teachers needs to be up close to students' initial attempts, making sure that they are building confidence and not making too many errors. This is a common weakness with 'less effective teachers'. Guided practice requires close supervision and feedback.
High success rate — in questioning and practice — is important. Rosenshine suggests the optimum is 80% i.e. high! Not 95-100% (too easy). He even suggests 70% is too low.

Independent, monitored practice. Successful teachers make time for students to do the things they've been taught, by themselves... when they're ready. *"Students need extensive, successful, independent practice in order for skills and knowledge to become automatic."*

(If you like the images in this post, they were created by Oliver Caviglioli and can be found on his website olicav.com

# The Final Word on Rosenshine's Principles on Instruction.

## Isn't it Just Common Sense?

This seems to be the most common response from teachers after reading Rosenshine's paper for the first time.

Well, yes and no.

That's the beauty of it.

My initial response to it was "I already know that I do it already"

But...

When I thought about my teaching, I saw that I hadn't really thought about my methods for a while, so I started mapping out a few lessons with Rosenshine's work in mind.

**I was surprised by how my teaching improved.**

It may seem like the things we do every day anyway but there is more to it than that (in my opinion). To me, it provides familiar ideas but presents them in a way that allows me to pick and choose the best principles to teach the differing ideas in Science.

That said, it is universally relevant for any subject.

Since I have been using Rosenshine's principles, I have found that less of my teaching time is wasted, my lessons have become more efficient and students have been making more progress.

But, just remember, it's not a checklist!

I like to see it as a toolbox, I select the right tool for the job resulting in the job being completed more efficiently.

**You wouldn't eat soup with a fork, would you? You could, but it would take ages!**

I urge you to read [Rosenshine's Principles of instruction](#) paper and then look at one the topics you teach and see how you could map it using the 10 principles.

Also, Sherrington's book is a must-read. You can read my [review of "Rosenshine's principles in action"](#) or if you trust me, you could just go and buy it [here if you are in the UK](#) or [here if you are in the US](#).

# Cognitive Load Theory.

If only we knew how students mentally process new information?

Oh, wait...

We do!

Cognitive Load Theory unlocks exactly how students (well, everyone actually) learn new information. Why it isn't the first thing taught to new teachers bewilders me!

Wanna know all about it?

I thought so, let's dive in.

## What is Cognitive Load Theory?

[Cognitive load theory](#) builds on the premise that working (or short-term) memory has a limited capacity and that overloading it reduces the effectiveness of teaching. Much in the same way that having too many windows open on your computer, reduces its capability to work properly.

Given that the goal of learning is to move new information from the working memory into the long term memory, Cognitive load theory suggests that instructional materials and environments should be designed to reduce this load, thus removing distractions enables a more efficient passage of the desired learning from working memory to the long term memory.

Cognitive Load Theory was initially developed by Psychologist, John Sweller in 1988 (*[Cognitive Load During Problem Solving: Effects on Learning](#)*), with further work done in 1998 (*[Cognitive Architecture and Instructional Design](#)*).

## What is Working Memory?

The working memory is responsible for rapid perceptual and linguistic processing. Put simply, it works out what the new information is all about and whether to store it in long term memory or discard it.

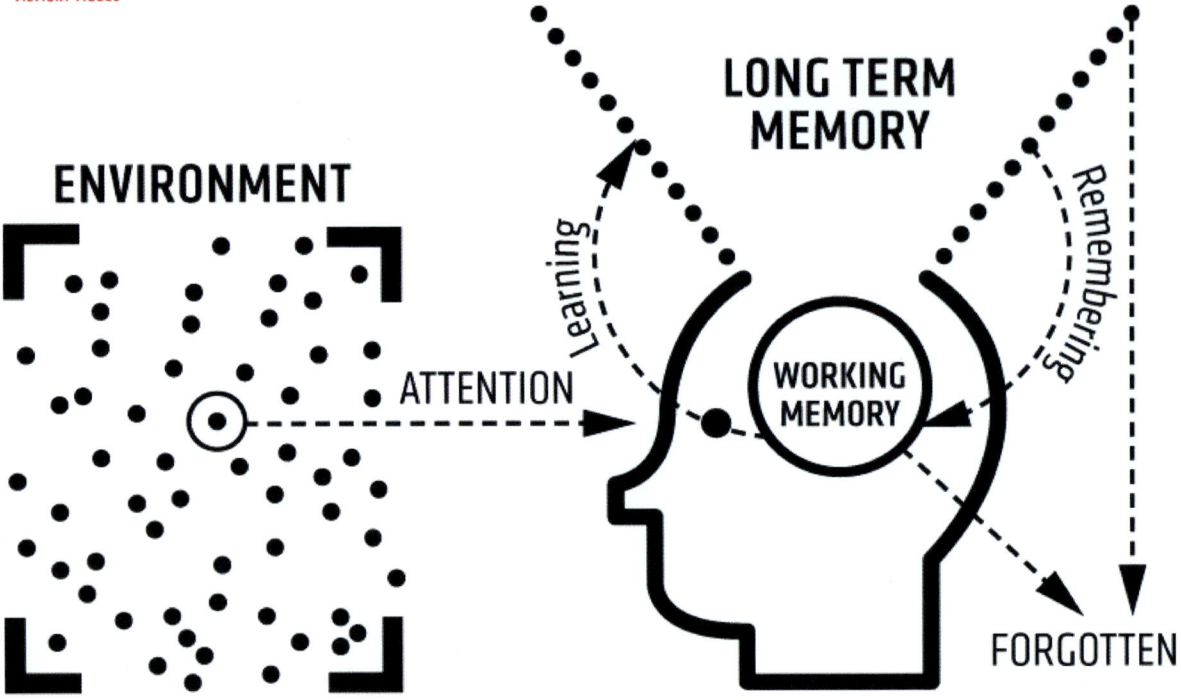

## What are Schemas?

When a student (or anyone for that matter) is subjected to new information, their brain gives it a classification and stores it in the long term memory, this classification is known as schemas.

Schemas are like folders in your memory where you store similar information, i.e. you may have a file for all things to do with clothes or things to do with pasta etc. You also have behavioural schemas. Those that store all things to do with driving a car, making a sandwich or ice skating.

The more you use these schemas (practice) the easier the retrieval of the knowledge. Schemas are a very big part of cognitive load theory.

## What is Cognitive Load?

Cognitive load refers to the amount of information the working memory can hold at any one given time. Most people can handle a cognitive load of between 3 and 7 separate pieces of information.

Cognitive load theory differentiates the types of cognitive load into 3 types; Intrinsic, Extraneous and Germane.

# What are the 3 Types of Cognitive Load?

The three types of cognitive load build upon each other, too much of each of the first two (Intrinsic and Extraneoous) may not leave enough working memory to deal with the third (Germane).

## Intrinsic Cognitive Load.

Intrinsic cognitive load refers to the innate difficulty of the task. For example, recalling that Clownfish live in anemones would be low intrinsic load, whereas, explaining why both species benefit from this would be a higher level of intrinsic load.

Teachers can match the intrinsic load of a topic to the experience of the learner but can't do much to reduce the complexity of the topic.

We can, however, reduce extraneous load.

## Extraneous Cognitive Load.

Extraneous cognitive load is where we as teachers have the most control.

Extraneous cognitive load is concerned with the material and environment we subject the students to.

Poorly constructed materials and busy classroom environments can lead to the split-attention effect and add to extraneous cognitive load, it is our job to reduce this with the way we present our lessons.

Simply stated the split-attention effect is the distraction generated by using too many conflicting principles. It is detrimental to cognitive load.

Reducing the materials down to only contain the elements that are required is crucial.

Irrelevant images, distracting sounds or animations or even fonts that are difficult to read, a monotone voice and complicated vocabulary all add to the extraneous load.

If you don't manage the first two correctly, the next one can't happen...

...and that's a BIG problem!

I bet you're wondering how you can reduce extraneous load right?

Don't worry we'll get to that in a bit.

**Germane Cognitive Load.**

Germane load is what we actually want to happen, it is the capacity of the working memory to link new ideas with information in the long term memory (It's the moment we've all seen, the "a-ha" lightbulb when a student finally gets it!).

The more prior knowledge a student has, the more effective the germane loading stage. Germane load is where [metacognitive strategies](#) come into play, it is where students are aware of their thinking processes and able to adapt new information accordingly.

Teaching students the prerequisite skills prior to having them undertake a more complicated task will help them construct new schemas that strengthen their working memory.

This means that pre-training, or teaching people prerequisite skills before introducing a more complex topic, will help them establish schemas that extend their working memory; and this then means that they can understand and learn more difficult information.

If we overload a student's working memory with intrinsic load (making the task too difficult to comprehend or carry out) or extraneous load (giving too many distracting stimuli), we don't leave enough to achieve the goal, the successful germane load.

This results in frustration (in both the student and the teacher) and a reduction in engagement in future tasks. How many times have you heard "I just don't get it, it won't stay in my head"?

Maybe analysing the intrinsic and extraneous load you are putting the students under needs a rethink.

## What are the 5 Principles of Reducing Cognitive Load?

I told you earlier when talking about extraneous load that I'd show you the best ways of reducing it. Well, as promised, here we go. (I'd never let you down!)

In his [2002 paper, Richard E. Mayer](#) described five principles that teachers can use to help reduce cognitive load and thus, increase retention and progress by our students.

As an exercise, take a look through a few of your lessons and ask yourself, "Do my lesson designs to follow these principles?".

# The Coherence Principle.

Quite simply, the coherence principle involves reducing the amount of information on each slide/page/worksheet to only that that is necessary.

Images, sounds and words that are not essential, add to cognitive load.

Giving the student's working memory fewer stimuli to focus on enables more processing power to be used by the germane load (remember this is our goal).

A fairly extreme example but it makes the correct point...reduce extraneous information!

## The Signalling Principle.

The signalling principle tells us to help our students focus on the information we are talking about by highlighting the important details.

We can do this via arrows or rings around the information. This reduces cognitive load by taking the work of scanning this visual away from the working memory.

This results in more juice for the germane load!

Winner!

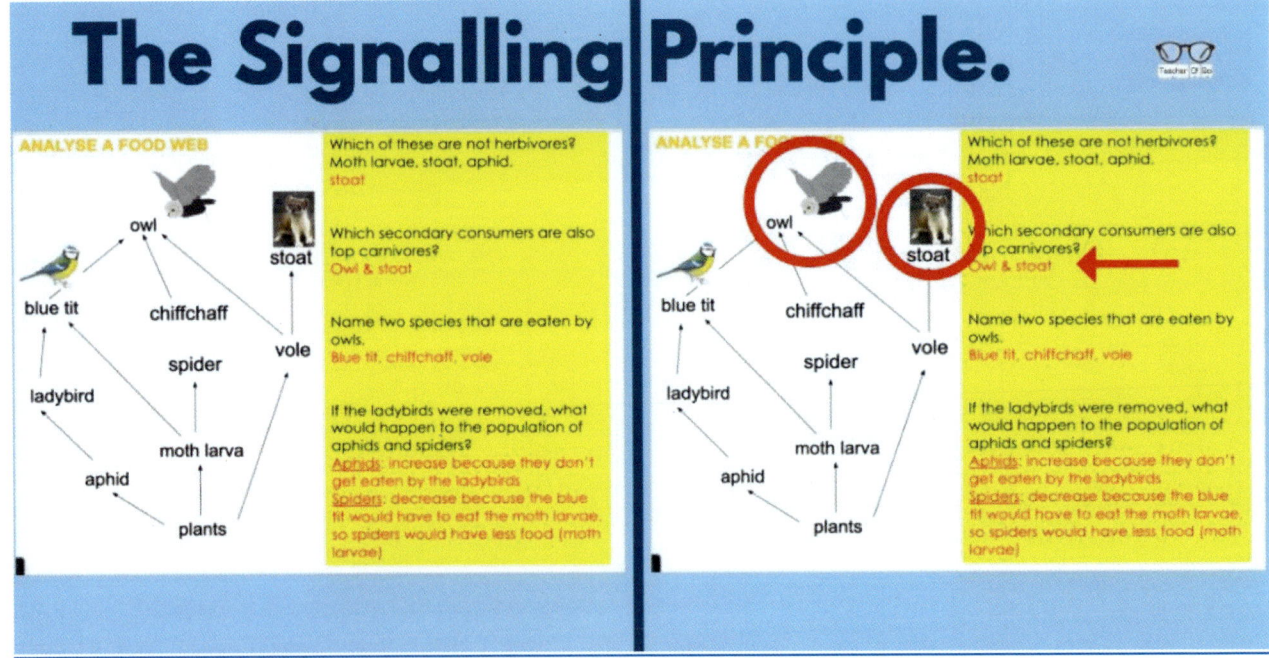

Imagine I'm talking to you about Question 2. Your eyes are immediately drawn to the highlighted areas, rather than having to waste cognitive load juice on scanning the page. Jackpot!

## The Redundancy Principle.

Students learn best from images and narration, rather than text and narration. Images (visual) and narration (audio) do not compete with each other, therefore they use less cognitive load.

This is known as the "Modality Effect".

Basically, don't put lots of text on your resources and definitely don't just read out the text word for word (you might as well tell your students to go to sleep, they're going to be doing that anyway!).

In John Sweller's original paper "*Cognitive Load Theory*" he concludes that, "Working memory capacity can be effectively increased, and learning improved, by using a dual-mode *presentation.*" (Cognitive Load Theory, 2011, Sweller, Ayres & Kalyuga).

Dual coding theory suggests that images, a small amount of text and narration (visual and verbal stimuli) are the most efficient way of reducing extraneous load. Just look at the two examples below that I have taken from Oliver Caviglioli's brilliant book "Dual Coding with Teachers"

### ACTIVITY 2

Jenny is head of the Humanities faculty. Fatima is the head of the History department. Tom, Joe and Sue work for Fatima. Harry is the head of the Geography department. Jo, Chaz and Tarnia report to Harry. Sue, Jo, Chaz and Harry are working together on the joint Modern Europe Project.

Who is the highest ranking person on the Modern Europe Project?

Which department has the most people on the Modern Europe project?

Which people are not involved with the Modern Europe project?

Confusing right? Lots of cognitive load wasted!

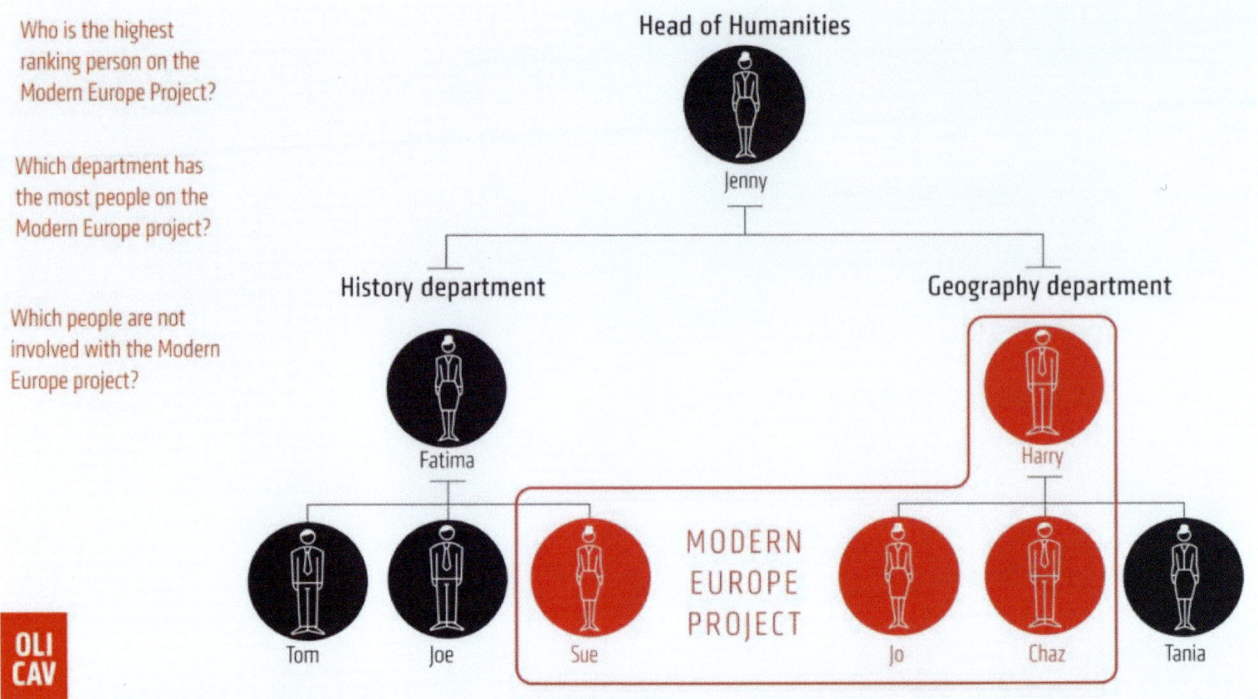

Much easier, right? Lots of germane load juice saved! (This image combines several of the 5 cognitive load reducing principles, can you spot them?

## Spatial Contiguity.

Placing labels next to the thing they are describing, so students don't have to waste cognitive load juice working anything out.

It's all about making the working memory's job easier in terms of intrinsic and extraneous load so students have more use of germane load; the ability to make those connections with previously learned information.

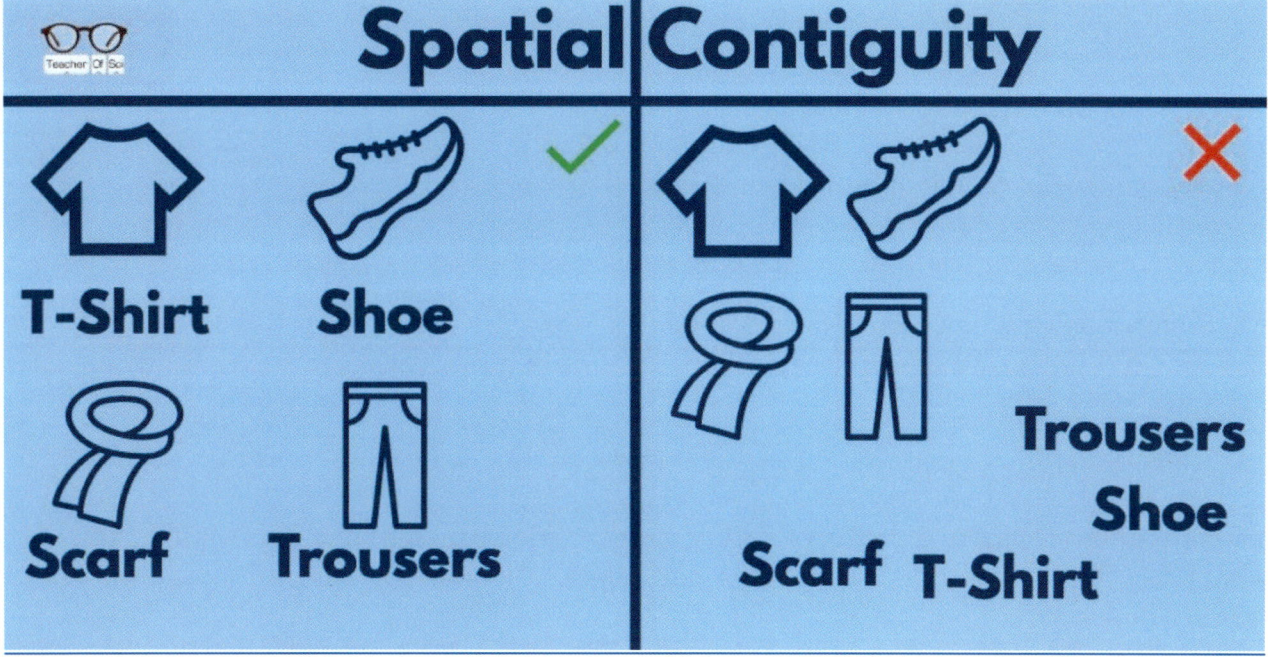

It may not seem like rocket science but you'd be surprised how many lessons you find this stuff in, I did (in some of my stuff). Check yours.

**Temporal Contiguity.**

Last but not least is temporal contiguity. This one is achieved simply by presenting the visual images and their labels at the same time. By doing this, the working memory knows they should be treated as an individual unit rather than separate entities.

# The Final Word on Cognitive Load Theory.

Now you see why I'm convinced Cognitive Load Theory should be taught to all trainee teachers. It literally teaches us how to teach!

Along with Rosenshine's Principles of Instruction, Metacognition and Dual Coding Theory, Cognitive Load Theory, in my opinion, should be the basis of all teacher training.

# Metacognition.

## What is Metacognition?

**How often do you reflect on your own thoughts and behaviours?**

As a colleague of mine recently put it to a group of assembled teachers:

'Think about how you got here today.

Have you been here before?

How did you choose which way to get here – method, route etc?'

**Metacognition refers to a person's ability to self-critique their approach to a task and adapt their behaviour to improve future outcomes. Often simply referred to as "Thinking about Thinking".**

Teaching metacognitive strategies to students improves their higher-order thinking and increases their ability to make maximum progress.

Effective teaching is the best way to improve outcomes, especially for disadvantaged students. The best teachers need a working knowledge and understanding of the most effective strategies in order to maximise the efficiency of their classrooms and the quality of the teaching and learning interactions therein.

By the end of this article, you may feel that you are "the converted" and you have been preached at; hopefully, no conversion is necessary if we all want to be effective teachers!

A lot of strategies that are now huddled under the umbrella of Metacognition and Self-Regulation are the same strategies many effective teachers have been employing, possibly in different guises or without conscious awareness in their classrooms for many years.

**ALEX QUIGLEY**
SENIOR ASSOCIATE: EDUCATION ENDOWMENT FOUNDATION

THE EVIDENCE-BASED CLASSROOM SERIES

# 7: METCOGNITION

Metacognition is part of the fabric of successful learning, but it can prove both complex and subtle. With understanding and planning, teachers can help pupils better appraise the metacognitive demands of the topics and tasks. Here is the EEF '6 Aspects of Metacognition' model that helps support teacher knowledge and planning so that they can mobilise metacognition in the classroom.

## METACOGNITIVE KNOWLEDGE

### KNOWLEDGE OF TASK

Having a thorough understanding of the task at hand, alongside clear goals, is essential for our pupils to learn effectively. Pupils can be prompted to consider how the task best relates to their prior knowledge. So, for example, if pupils are asked to translate a passage of German, they need to understand the act of translation, relating the task to their knowledge of the topic at hand, their

### KNOWLEDGE OF STRATEGIES

Being able to apply the right strategy in timely fashion for a given task in the classroom is essential for success. With more complex tasks, pupils will often be required to select a strategy with increasing independence. For example, in primary school, pupils undertaking long division in maths will select from strategies such as 'chunking', 'estimating', the 'bus stop method' etc. This selection can be modelled and guided

### KNOWLEDGE OF SELF

With every given task in the classroom, we draw upon our knowledge of ourselves as learners. That is to say, how have we responded and performed in similar tasks? How have similar tasks made us feel? For example, for a pupil undertaking spelling tests across a school term, their knowledge of self – spelling knowledge, preparation, emotion towards tests – becomes a critical aspect of them self-regulating

## THE MODEL

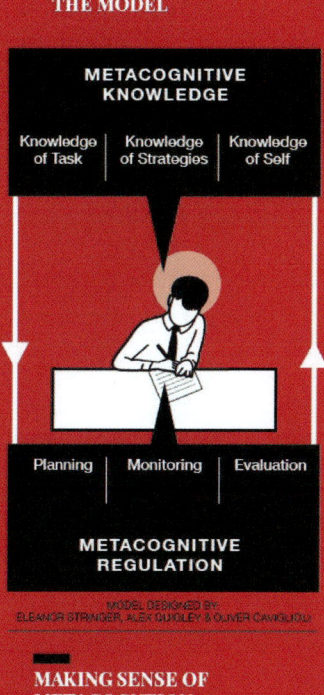

MODEL DESIGNED BY:
ELEANOR STRINGER, ALEX QUIGLEY & OLIVER CAVIGLIOLI

### MAKING SENSE OF METACOGNTION

The EEF has produced a helpful guidance report on 'Metacognition and Self-regulation' for teachers and school leaders (see: https://bit.ly/2HDv4Ak). This guidance is designed to support teachers to understand metacognition and self-regulation, before implementing a range of evidence-informed recommendations in the classroom

The guidance supports teachers to explicitly plan and monitor the development of metacognition in the classroom, via explicit instruction, metacognitive talk, modelling, or in supporting effective independent learning.

## METACOGNITIVE REGULATION

### PLANNING

Considering how to support pupils how to best plan – such as drawing upon their background knowledge, organise their resources, allocate their time – is common to every teacher.

For more complex tasks, such as planning a revision schedule, pupils will need explicit instruction & modelling of how to do this well. Planning prompts in this case

### MONITORING

Many pupils will recognise the need to plan for a given task, but once they have begun they fail to adequately monitor their progress or make changes when planned strategies prove ineffective. For example, pupils who are tackling an extended writing task can often fail to monitor their writing. Effective monitoring could involve self-questioning to check the writing is clear and addressing audience & purpose, or apprais-

### EVALUATION

Pupils are commonly expected to appraise their own effectiveness for a given task. We know however that pupils can poorly judge their learning – or fail to self-evaluate and reflect upon their successes and failures altogether. For example, a pupil completing a self-portrait in art may need to evaluate whether their strategies worked – such as using perspective, proportion, using mirror, hatching etc. With

Oliver Caviglioli | @olicav | teach | teachwire.net

# What is the research behind metacognition?

The term metacognition has been used to describe our own understanding of how we perceive, remember, think, and act, that is, what we know about what we know. (*Metacognition: Knowing about Knowing* edited by Janet Metcalfe and Arthur P. Shimamura (1994)).

## Thinking about Thinking.

Metacognitive knowledge is the knowledge of yourself as a learner – how you learn best; the strategies you have at your disposal; the tasks you have to complete and how you complete them.

**Metacognitive strategies help us plan, monitor and evaluate our learning.**

Metacognition as a concept is nothing new, the term itself was first coined in the 1970s by John Flavell. Over the years there has been much debate around the precise definition and the component parts.

## Piaget's Influence.

In 1963, Flavell was the first to publish in English a study on the research and work of Piaget (*The Developmental Psychology of Jean Piaget*), from this, the science of cognitive development was born.

Looking back with the perspective we now have; the work of Lev Vygotsky on his Zone of Proximal Development, specifically the transition from a learner being directed by a "more knowledgeable other" to the learner becoming capable of understanding their own cognitive abilities would be considered metacognitive development.

Essentially, Metacognition is the ability we have to use our existing knowledge to plan strategies for approaching tasks, take necessary steps to problem solve, reflect on and evaluate results, and modify our approaches as required.

In an excellent article in the most recent copy of Impact Magazine for the CCT James Mannion defines it as 'monitoring and controlling your thought processes'.

Mannion also urges us to be careful around the over-simplification of the concept; however, we can distil the basics.

# Metacognitive Strategies in Education

Metacognition is one of the aspects students need in order to become self-regulated learners; it is important to remember that developing the former does not automatically create the latter.

Before setting off on anything classroom-based that you call a 'metacognitive strategy' you must have a basic grasp of the ways students develop their own metacognitive skills as a learner, and you must model these in your own practice.

**Don't fall into the trap of designing generic or explicit 'Metacognition Lessons' or 'Study Skills' sequences.**

Embed the concepts more deeply in your subject-specific practice and focus on wanting the students to be more effective independent learners, reflecting on their approaches and regulating their behaviour appropriately to ensure maximum success and optimised outcomes.

## Why is metacognition important?

One of the key conclusions drawn by the National Academy of Sciences in their "*How People Learn II*" report from 2018 is that "*Successful learning requires coordination of multiple cognitive processes that involve different networks in the brain. In order to coordinate these processes, an individual needs to be able to monitor and regulate his own learning. The ability to monitor and regulate learning changes over the life span and can be improved through interventions*".

The EEF Guidance Report tells us that evidence and research suggest 7 months+ of progress "when used well" and that there is a lot of potential, "particularly for disadvantaged students".

"When used well" is key, as is "potential"; we need to ensure that strategies and interventions designed to promote metacognitive awareness in students are supported by professional development for teachers.

Teachers should be guided in how best to embed these strategies into their classroom environments and day-to-day teaching and learning interactions.

These ideas around appropriate implementation are explored Joke vanVelzenin in "*Metacognitive Learning; Advancing Learning by Developing General Knowledge of the Learning Process*".

"In today's schools, most students are taught how to summarize, take notes, and read for understanding, though mostly without specifically being taught how to figure out by themselves when and why these learning techniques can be most effective.

Without obtaining a thorough understanding of the reasons behind the effectiveness of learning techniques, in that general knowledge of the learning process is being developed, learning can be hindered and become unnecessarily difficult, particularly, where new and unfamiliar learning tasks are concerned.

This makes the development of general knowledge of the learning process essential for lifelong learning."

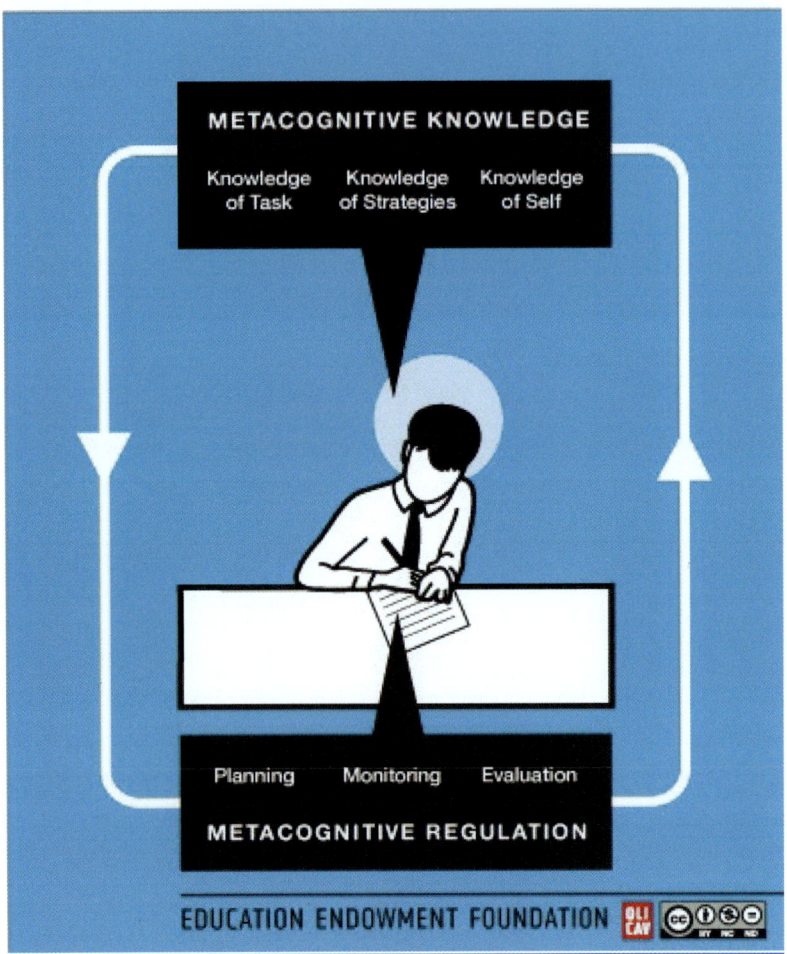

## Metacognition in the Classroom

The EEF report is keen to point out to us that much less is known about effective implementation of metacognitive strategies in the classroom.

However, we can group together a range of approaches and opportunities that relate well to encouraging students to develop their metacognitive awareness.

One area where we can have immediate success is in the creation and management of appropriate resources. Encouraging students to use them effectively, thoughtfully and productively; this latter phrase encapsulates the metacognitive approach nicely.

## So, what can we try?

### Retrieval Practice.

When done well and used appropriately retrieval practices help activate prior knowledge, ascertain prior knowledge and also give students practice at using previously learnt material effectively.

Thus speeding up the cognitive transfer from long-term to [working memory](#) and therefore embedding the learning more deeply.

### Problem Solving.

Worked examples and problem pairs are just a couple of examples of how modelling and articulating the process of using knowledge helps students better understand how to apply the range of metacognitive strategies.

We can also, as teachers make sure that we use questions to allow students to develop their reasoning and explain their answers. We can stimulate debate, press for depth and 'design better conversations' for learning.

### Backwards Fading and Progressive Modelling.

Both of these strategies can help students to the correct process by holding their hand through it in the first instance then gradually removing the level of support until the process becomes more natural and 'automatic'.

**Does this remind you of anyone?**

**Vygotsky perhaps!**

If we adopt [Rosenshine's suggestions](#) around introducing new material in small steps we ensure that we do not overload student working memory and we, therefore, do not hinder performance.

The end goal as a teacher is to fade ourselves and the resources away at an appropriate speed until students reach the level of performance that allows for proper independence.

### This cannot and should not be done too quickly!

As well as the tools required to complete the task we can (and should) also teach the management of the task and which strategies are most effective in which situations.

In order to further the support that moves students towards independent and 'self-regulated' learning, we should ensure that we are designing those appropriate resources.

Resources that are streamlined, efficient and uncomplicated; ones that show an understanding of [cognitive load](#) and student working memory.

# 7 Examples of Metacognitive Questions Students Should ask Themselves.

1. **What should I do first?**
2. **Is something confusing me?**
3. **Could I explain this to someone else?**
4. **Do I need help to understand this?**
5. **Where did I go wrong?**
6. **Does this relate to other situations or prior knowledge?**
7. **How can I do it better?**

## Metacognition Strategies.

We can try getting students to reflect and evaluate their own learning experiences more with simple prompts:

-What concepts from today's class did you find difficult to understand?

-Specifically, what will you do to improve your understanding of the concepts that were difficult?

We can also support students with their resource management. We can give them a range of well-taught and modelled study strategies that they can choose from when revising, for example; flashcards, MCQs, elaboration, self-quizzing and concept maps.

Giving them a well-structured study guide, they can work on what strategies work best for them.

### Metacognition in action!

We can then ask them to articulate the success (or not) of their independent study to help them identify those strategies that are working and those that are not.

**By setting goals and monitoring progress towards them, students become more aware of their own thinking and learning.**

Perkins' four levels of Metacognitive Learner (1992) can be a really useful template for not only identifying the different needs of students but also then enabling more focussed and targeted intervention and support.

## The Metacognition Cycle.

1. Assess the task.
2. Evaluate strengths and weaknesses.
3. Plan the approach.
4. Apply strategies.
5. Reflect.

# Metacognition in CPD (Continuing Professional Development).

As mentioned earlier, institutions themselves need to recognise the potential of appropriately designed interventions to support metacognition.

**In my view, this starts at the top and with the teachers themselves.**

Focussed, evidence-informed professional learning opportunities that are iterative and delivered by those with the appropriate knowledge, supported by frameworks and discussion models that help coach and develop staff delivery.

Simply ascribing a school's 'metacognitive approach' to the creation of a one-off generic Study Skills programme will not be effective.

The approach needs to be outward-facing and collegiate, with staff collaborating on the delivery of strategy as well as assessing its impact, perhaps in small focussed Learning Groups.

When embarking on any form of action research in this way it will be key to ensure that the parameters are clear and precise and that there is a concrete idea of what 'success' looks like i.e. how its impact can be measured otherwise.

As with all CPD, be aware of the needs of those in the room and their own skills. How 'novice' are they? What support do they need? If teachers can develop and improve their own metacognition then they are better equipped to help develop it in others.

We need to distil the complexity of metacognition into steps that students and teachers can understand; as novice learners, we are initially poor in making judgements about our own learning, and as with anything our expertise increases over time and through experience.

## The Final Word on Metacognition.

If we want students to be able to become truly independent learners and to be able to think for themselves, we must teach them to think in a metacognitive way.

We don't need to make huge changes to what we do, just tweak our teaching to set them up with the self-reflective questioning techniques.

# Dual Coding Theory.

This section was written for me by [Oliver Caviglioli](#), author of *"Dual Coding With Teachers"*..

## Allan Paivio and his Dual Coding Theory.

Back in 1971, Canadian researcher, Allan Paivio, formulated his dual coding theory. And then spent the next four decades researching it, trying to 'break it'.

**He didn't manage it.**

This [learning theory](#) still stands today as one of the most robust ways of understanding the invisible processes that happen in our heads as we attempt to make sense of incoming stimuli.

**His most significant discovery was that we have two separate channels that deal with verbal and visual stimuli.**

While being independent of each other, they are also able to create what Paivio called "associative connections" between them. So, they are both apart from one another but can cooperate in forming linked pairs of words and images.

By forming such a link, the encoding process is enriched. It leaves a double memory trace and, in the words of Professor [Paul Kirschner](#), results in "double-barrelled learning" because of the resultant double opportunity of being retrieved by either verbal or visual means.

## Dual Coding Theory, Supported by Cognitive Load Theory.

Encoding, of course, is psychologists' term for learning and, so, such a powering up of the encoding and retrieval processes deserves teachers' close attention. It's no surprise then that John Sweller —the originator of the related [Cognitive Load Theory](#)— concludes that, "Working memory capacity can be effectively increased, and learning improved, by using a dual-mode *presentation.*" (Cognitive Load Theory, 2011, Sweller, Ayres & Kalyuga)

Often, cognitive science brings bad news to students. They are confronted by the facts that learning happens through thinking hard (Coe), that the comforting habit of rereading and highlighting is very inefficient, and that studying one topic at a time is less than optimal. Dual coding is quite different in that pairing words and images don't incur any additional cognitive load and also greatly helps retrieval. It's a 'freebie'.

**But, as good as this news is, it's only half the story.**

When Paivio found that the two channels worked as separate systems, he also noted that they were also fundamentally different in structure. Verbal information, you won't be surprised to learn, is sequential in construction. Words are joined together in "concatenation" as philosopher, [Bertrand Russell](), described it when comparing the relative merits of text and diagrams in conveying meaning.

## The Importance of Visuals in Education.

Visual information was defined by Paivio as being synchronous, or simultaneous' in structure. These two synonymous terms were used to explain that with diagrams, several, if not all, the elements could be viewed in one go. Words, by contrast, have to be processed one at a time.

While Paivio noted these important structural differences, he didn't devote his research to exploring them much further. Others did, I'm glad to say, and we will shortly meet them and learn what they discovered. But, for now, we'll stay with Paivio's studies of the associative links between the two modality systems.

As robust as his findings were over several decades, we ought not to forget that the nature of the content learned by his laboratory subjects was cognitively unchallenging. Like Ebbinghaus in the century before him, Paivio used simple content in order to discount any element of comprehension messing his pure work on retrieval.

**That's not how schools work though, they do deal with cognitively challenging content.**

The knowledge organiser with its lists of facts —let's acknowledge it—while a very useful document, hardly represents the apex of schools' intellectual aspirations. Instead, different approaches are needed to mesh together such isolated facts into coherent networks and integrated concepts.

## The Visual Argument (Larkin and Simon).

That's where Jill Larkin and Herbert Simon come into the picture. In 1987, they wrote a paper that developed Paivio's distinction of sequential and synchronous information structures.

By comparing the time, effort and accuracy involved in understanding concepts communicated in either verbal or visual format, they arrived at what is now called The Visual Argument. In their study, well-constructed diagrams were judged to be more computationally efficient than text.

Behind this somewhat technical term, lies this reasoning. Because of the sequential nature of verbal information, each word is addressed one at a time. That, of course, isn't all that's entailed. To make sense of each word, they need to relate to others.

Sometimes this is simply the ones directly preceding them. But others may well be further apart in a previous phrase or sentence. Such distances require cognitive effort in searching and connecting in order to make the necessary inferences to make sense of the text as a whole.

**Diagrams don't work that way!**

Constituent parts of a diagram are all significant, unlike the words in a piece of text. In addition, these visual elements can be perceived in one go, and not serially.

This is why Paivio described visual information being synchronous or simultaneous in structure. And this is why psychologists argue ([Clark & Lyons 2004](#)) that diagrams can be largely understood by using our everyday perception.

## Graphics for Learning.

Gestalt psychology, for nearly a century, has shown us that we immediately understand that proximity of elements represent commonality, as indeed does inclusion within a border (think Euler and Venn diagrams). These natural capacities are at play in the reading of diagrams and require considerably less cognitive resources than in reading texts.

The two cognitive, or computational, tasks that are more efficient with diagrams are the reduced need to search for relevant items within sentences and, correspondingly, the easier use of inference because [metacognition](#) is able to take place.

**Put simply...**

Reading texts involves an almost constant travelling back and forth searching which parts relate to which. This, then, makes inferences so much more difficult, or effortful, to make.

The example below, that I use in my presentations to make the concept of computational efficiency come alive, makes the point more effectively than my explanations.

Let's look again at the images we saw earlier in the Cognitive Load Theory Section.

*From the text on the left, try and answer the questions. Difficult isn't it!*

## ACTIVITY 2

Jenny is head of the Humanities faculty. Fatima is the head of the History department. Tom, Joe and Sue work for Fatima. Harry is the head of the Geography department. Jo, Chaz and Tarnia report to Harry. Sue, Jo, Chaz and Harry are working together on the joint Modern Europe Project.

Who is the highest ranking person on the Modern Europe Project?

Which department has the most people on the Modern Europe project?

Which people are not involved with the Modern Europe project?

*Now try to answer the same questions by looking at the image below...*

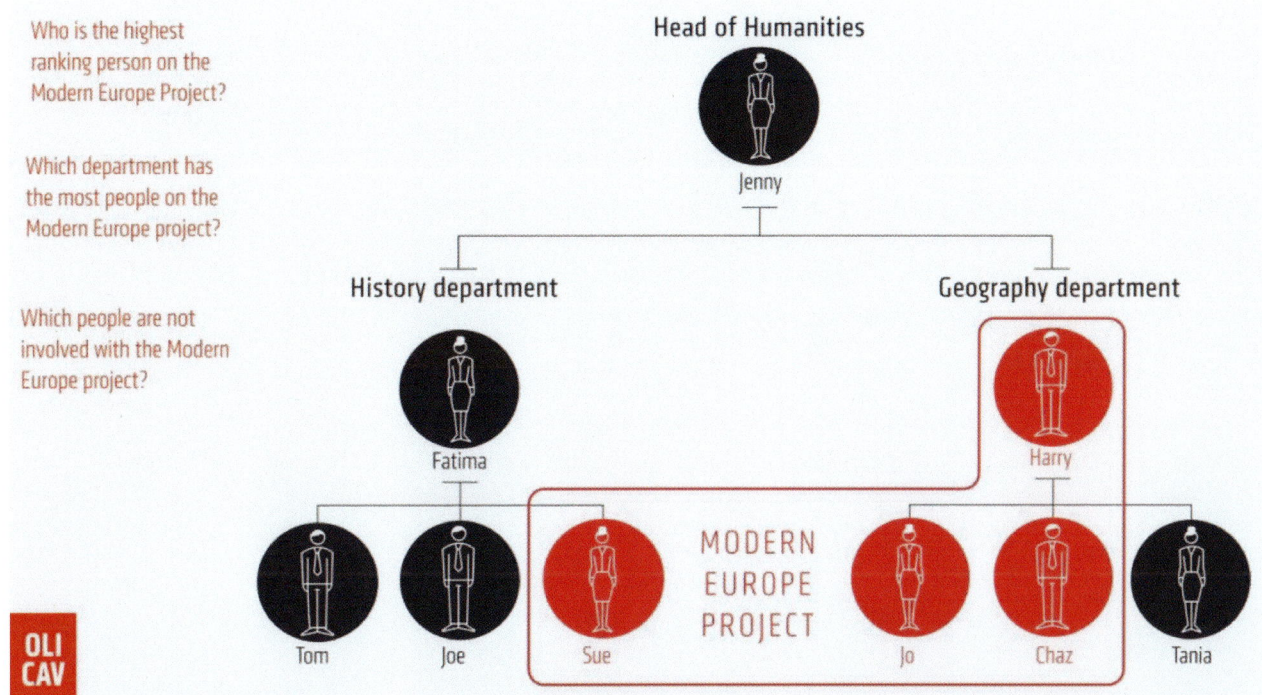

*Much easier right?*

Convinced of this you may be but, as always, there's more to it than just presenting a diagram to your students.

As cognitive science authors, Clark and Lyons (2004) warn: "**Visuals ignored, don't teach**".

It's all very well to give your students diagrams that convey information that require less effort to understand, but if you don't then use them to make your students think, not much will be learned.

**Diagrams should be thought of as platforms from which to better analyse texts and prepare for speaking and writing.**

And then there are other problems to overcome. The Visual Argument only happens when teachers have chosen an appropriate visual tool. Exploring the differences between rural and urban settings is not best represented by a timeline for example. And plotting the plot of Hamlet becomes confusing if a mind map is used.

## Deductive Reasoning in Dual Coding Theory.

Graphic organisers can usefully be grouped along these four types of deductive reasoning: defining, comparing, sequencing and linking cause and effect. Identifying the nature of the knowledge task is essential before moving on to choose an appropriate visual tool.

As you might now expect, there's one more danger to avoid. Supposing the correct organiser is chosen to fit the nature of the task, its execution needs to be adequate.

Clark and Lyons (2004) highlight poor execution as a major factor behind dual coding's diminished impact. Above all, teachers need to make their handwriting legible. To be confident of this, printing in a clear, bold style with no flourishes or elaborations, is essential.

Forcing students to decipher a rushed handwritten script is an unnecessary cognitive burden that clearly bears an extraneous, unproductive load.

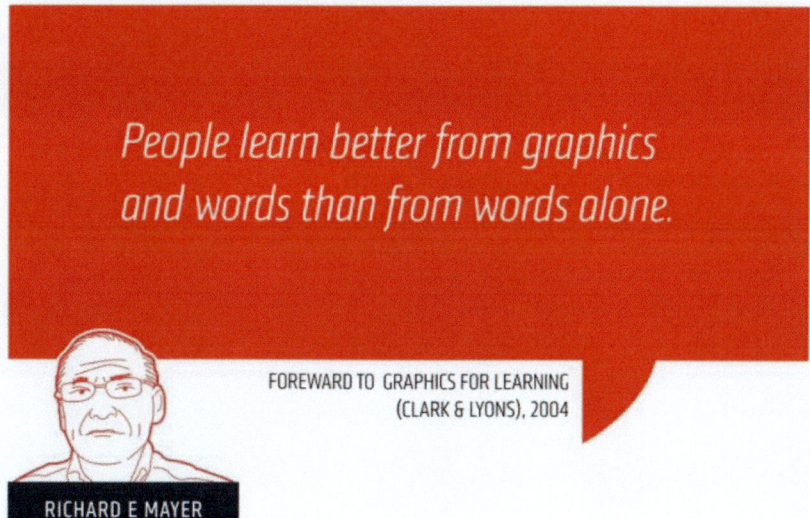

Other graphic considerations when creating dual coded communications involve the following four principles I devised after responding to requests for feedback from teachers on Twitter.

**Firstly...**

Simply to cut—reduce the volume presented on page or slide. It's the easiest and most effective of all the principles.

**Next...**

Chunk the selected content. Identify the categories so it's easier to make sense. And signal the chunks by providing more headings than you normally would.

**Then..**

Aligning the chunks, and any other element on the page —line or image— makes scanning and search so much easier for the reader. In other words, don't make them 'artistic' and random in placement. Order makes reading and scanning so very much easier.

**Finally...**

And lastly, continuing on the non-artistic perspective, practice restraint in the number and intensity of colours used, along with the use of a single typeface (font) ensuring it isn't a fancy, hard-to-read display font or Comic Sans. Typographers have a long history of theory, research and practice as to what makes reading easy.

**Just look closely at any newspaper or magazine design and you will see these principles in action.**

# Conclusion.

There you have it.

In my opinion, these are the strategies we should be teaching new teachers and using ourselves.

I hope you found these strategies thought provoking.

I challenge you to use a bit of metacognition and reflect on your own teaching practice and start using evidence based practices in your classroom.

Please feel free to get in touch with any feedback or suggestions you have.
paul@teacherofsci.com

Printed in Poland
by Amazon Fulfillment
Poland Sp. z o.o., Wrocław